Redefine, Reinvest, Renew

It's Your Time

K Adonica Dillon —

Joy, Peace & Prosperity!

LaShell Williams

LaShell Williams

Printed in the United States by Morris Publishing®
3212 East Highway 30
Kearney, NE 68847
1-800-650-7888

Contents

Acknowledgments 4

Introduction 5

Chapter 1 Your Life 7

Chapter 2 What, Why and Who 27

Chapter 3 What Do You Really Want or Need Next 43

Chapter 4 Redefine Based on Your Reality 65

Chapter 5 Control Your Controllables 79

Chapter 6 Create Your Happy Even in the Storm 93

Chapter 7 Renew You 107

Progress Tracker 123

Resource Guide 125

Acknowledgments

First and foremost, I thank my Father God for mercy, grace, protection, strength, motivation, favor, elevated faith and life.

Mother, Loretta
Thank you for life, love, lessons and ongoing unwavering support. You have always believed in me, encouraged me beyond many valleys and steadfastly covered me with endless prayers. I love you beyond words Queen Diva.

Son, Lawreese
Thank you for motivating me all of these years with the gift and responsibility of being your mother. You inspired me to achieve, grow and overcome obstacles so that I could be there for you. I love you infinitely and look forward to many more happy chapters.

Grandmothers, Mamie and Merlee
Thank you for my parents and life through you. Your journey in church truly inspired my spiritual growth from childhood. Thank you for also covering me through your intercessory prayers. I love you.

Family, Saint Philip Church Family, Diva Circle and Friends
Thank you for being there for me throughout various seasons. You know what "role you play in my life" and I truly appreciate the love, support, prayers, talks, laughs and experiences throughout the years.

Editor, Angela P. Moore-Thorpe of APM Public Relations
Thank you for your support, insight, great services and professionalism. You are truly gifted above and beyond.

Introduction

Do you ever find yourself feeling behind schedule, delaying life-changing goals, defeated, somewhat lost, overwhelmed, frustrated, disgusted, disconnected or simply not content with the page you are on in your life right now? Stop beating yourself up and join the national club. Did a major life event or change from the past or recently cause you to detour from your Purpose? To others, you may appear to have it all together or like you don't have a care in the world. However, your reality may be that deep down inside, you may feel like you are just not doing enough or be where you should be by now. You are headed in the right direction for even laying eyes on this page, whether you are considering this book for yourself or someone you care about. On your daily, weekly and monthly To Do List, you may be either last or not on the list at all. If the previous statement pertains to you, let's start the process of correcting that today. I can relate first hand because I have been there and done that a few times. For years, I was not even on my own list but my family, friends, church, community organizations, associations and coworkers were. I put everyone ahead of myself the majority of the time. Others were happy or satisfied when I was there for them, but I was not there for myself and eventually it began to take a toll on me. While some groups and people on my list were happy because they were taken care of, I was drained, tired or angry because I kept postponing myself. However, the reality is that it was my own fault. Can you relate to this? If you are not careful, you will start resenting some groups or people because you are stretched thin, and it is not even their fault in some cases. You have the ability and power to manage your life differently although your plate may be full with responsibilities and overwhelming demands. As you read this, you may be thinking to yourself that this Author just don't know your story and not realistic. It is true that I do not know your story, but I do know about long-term risk of not putting yourself at the top of your list or allowing a major life change to define you. It is time to reprioritize and redefine yourself. When you do reprioritize, the rest of your list will have a better outcome. Keep reading and working this book experience because I have a newsflash and this book will help you, to help yourself for an overdue change. It may be late, but later is better than never. It does not matter how educated, uneducated, financially successful, financially challenged or who you may be or where you come from; you must be first on your list after God. It is easier said than done but it can be done and this book journey will help guide and empower you to do just that with a realistic and personable, step-by-step action plan. You may have already accomplished allot, or be in the middle of some major success not realizing that you can enjoy it even more with a slight adjustment. Are you ready? Get out of your own way starting today. You may be asking yourself what that really means for you. Well, we will explore that and break it down to fit your situation, circumstances or season. *It is a new week, a new day and a new hour. Redefine, reinvest and renew....let's move into your 3R experience.*

Chapter 1

Your Life

"Are you on your own daily schedule?"

Life is a very interesting journey with many seasons, some that you did not anticipate or welcome. That is where the common saying of "Life happens" comes into play. Regardless of where you are in life, remember that it is a blessing to still be on this side of the ground. As long as you are still here, you have a chance to start over or go to the next level. We all may be different, but we are the same when it comes right down to some facts. Most of what happens in life is not in our control but our reaction is. We cannot pick which circumstances to be born into. We all have imperfections, we all want to be accepted or validated, we all have fears and we all are on some type of journey taking a different route. So many people waste time judging or disliking who or what they do not understand instead of growing and seeking knowledge. Most of how and who you are, is learned or stemmed from your environment. We are not all equipped the same, but we face similar struggles. This book is designed to meet you wherever you are as you decide where you are going next. As you may have already discovered, most of your life outcomes are from your reaction or inaction. You may have regrets concerning your health, personal life, finances, education or career. You may be stuck or trying to get past minor or major changes. Remember to be patient with yourself and that nothing long-term happens overnight even with all of the *prayer* in world. Did your situation or detour happen overnight? The solution, breakthrough and answer won't either, but if you stay on top of it, eventually it will. Regardless of your age and background, you have probably discovered that life is not quite what you envisioned or planned for yourself. Even if you are successful, you may be disappointed that your success does not complete all areas of your life that are important to you. Know that although you may think that nobody understands how you may feel, the majority of people that are not living in denial are in a similar place within. Are you dealing with change, a situation or detour? We will refer to yours as "it". Although this may sound obvious, it's crucial to acknowledge "it" for what "it" is and how you feel about whatever "it" is. Perhaps "it" is a family member that betrayed or hurt you, failed relationship, a child that got off track despite your best efforts, job without future growth, stressful career, high school or college drop-out, discrimination, ongoing financial challenges, weight issues, depression, jealousy, low self-esteem, internal void, addiction, self-doubt, insecurity, loneliness, anger or something else that may be weighing you down. Most of us are dealing with more than one of these issues and we cannot afford to dwell on everything that may not be right. However, you must acknowledge anything that takes a

> *Be honest with yourself. You will not be at PEACE until you face the truth. Peace is priceless.*

toll on you daily or weekly. There are some things that you do not have any control over and you have to keep it moving and just shake it off. You need to deal with your "it" if you find that your "it" is constantly on your mind throughout the week or month, makes you angry or discouraged. Even if you tried to deal with it before and failed, try again until you overcome or conquer it. Remember that you owe it to yourself even if you do not feel like facing or working on your "it". Be completely honest with yourself even if the truth stinks or is ugly. Look at this as confidential self-surgery because it is between you and God. Do not be hard on whatever you discover about yourself during this journey because most of us are who we are based on our background, DNA and environment which is often times, beyond our control. While we must be accountable, it is important to identify the root of some emotions or challenges. For example, if you are struggling financially, it is fair to assume that your parents also struggled because wealth and lack of wealth seems to transfer to the next generation unfortunately. However, many people are better off than their parents due to the sacrifices in their parents' generation. Many people have better opportunities younger and more options as they should since the next generation is progressive. Whatever "it" is has a root and you can shape your life better when you can identify this. You may have wrestled with "it" on and off or think you overcame "it" but may surprisingly facing it again. Within this chapter, you will have space and a chance to roll up your sleeves to dissect what is going on in your life beneath the surface. The answers and solutions are deep within you. Meanwhile, ask yourself the following and revisit this later in the Tracker portion of this book:

1. What is your "it" or "its"?

   _____

   _____

   _____

2. How has "it" affected you?

_____

_____

_____

3. What have you done about "it" in the past?

_____

_____

_____

4. What are you going to do about your "it"?

_____

_____

_____

5. How do you ignore or make excuses for "it"?

_____

_____

_____

6. Is there a relative, friend or co-worker that caused or contributed to your "it"?

_____

_____

_____

7. What are you going to do about roots or enablers?

_____

_____

_____

8. Why do you want to do something about "it" now?

_____

_____

_____

9. How would conquering "it" improve your life?

_____

_____

_____

10. How can you commit to yourself to handle "it"?

_____

_____

_____

Please do not allow the list of questions to overwhelm you and do not get distracted on just one question. You will be able to revisit and work on this portion later but it is important to start the thought process about these questions as you move through this life-changing experience. At some point, you may feel uncomfortable or emotional somehow as you explore some questions and chapters, and that is necessary. It just means that you are truly working the process and that you soon will have a realistic and attainable, success bound action plan. A few general and very common "its" that hold some people back are failed relationships (dating, friends or family), insecurity and finances. Most of who we are and how we view or handle the following four areas is usually based on what we observed or experienced early on in life. Although I cannot address your individual situation, the following are steps that were highly effective for experts and myself. Perhaps you will discover something that will assist you as you improve, start or continue what you desire.

Insecurity/Self Doubt

You may have it going on overall, and that is great if you do. Regardless of how successful or overall confident you may be, you may find yourself missing out on even more in life because of fear which is a part of insecurity. Insecurity is defined as uncertainty or anxiety about oneself; lack of confidence.

If we are completely honest, we all are insecure about at least one area of ourselves or our life. It is an issue when our uncertainty, anxiety or self-doubt limits us from getting to the next level within our life or keeps us paralyzed in an unhealthy situation at home or work. It is easier to just avoid uncomfortable topics or issues but eventually most things will get worse or make you

13

unhappy, depressed, self-destructive or struggle indefinitely. Again, most self-doubt or insecurity is linked to something from childhood or society. If your insecurity is internal, it may stem from not being encouraged, complimented, acknowledged or rewarded as a child while you noticed other children were at school, home or within society. Or even as an adult,

> *Do not let self-doubt, insecurities or fear of change allow repeated offenses. You deserve respect.*

you have noticed that for whatever reason you are treated differently in school or at work. Over time, this may have affected you subconsciously. Some small part of you may not feel worthy of the promotion, the confidence to start your own business, the right to demand more respect within your personal relationship and other areas that you silently just tolerate. While you may think this is not a big deal right now, it will be a big deal later if it continues and contribute to your insecurities and decreased happiness. Realistically, whatever you are dealing with may take awhile to resolve but you owe it to yourself to face it head on. Do not let self-doubt, insecurities or fear of change allow repeated offenses. You deserve respect.

Relationships

You have to teach people how to treat you. People can only get away with what you allow or accept. You may currently respond to indifference based on what you observed the majority of your life. Regardless of your conflict resolution background, two-way communication is the most effective long-term method. Someone may have offended you without even realizing it. Give people the benefit of the doubt in most situations and let them know that you were surprised or disappointed about what they said or did in a none confrontational tone. Once you have informed the person, it is their responsibility to avoid repeating the same offense. Hopefully, they appreciate you sharing your feelings, and avoid repeating the offense. If they continue, you should revisit the subject one last time or give them consequences like distancing yourself, simply not responding or if it is extreme----cut them off. For more serious situations, you may have to take more drastic measures accordingly if it relates to the workplace, school or relatives. The bottom line is you have control most of the time on how you are treated; although, addressing the situation may be uncomfortable or require change. The truth is that we give other people too much power sometimes just to keep the peace. If you are not at peace within yourself, then there really is no true peace long term. Is the person valuable enough for you to still be affected? Your answer is probably yes if the person is a parent, spouse, child or other close relative. If they are outside of that circle, you may have to really think about the question deeper. In life, sometimes we have to distance ourselves from people that are detractors or mostly negative. The ideal situation would be to communicate about the situation and start anew. However, after fairly communicating and making an honest effort to make things work, you may have to cut your losses and move forward without that person in your routine or life. Some people confuse communication with confrontation. No two people will ever view everything exactly the same. It is natural to have disagreements and people should be mature enough to talk it out. Get it on the table, communicate respectfully, apologize if necessary, release it and move forward. If both parties cannot, then obviously more growth is pending within at least one of them if not both. One mistake that holds many people back from resolution is their stubborn motive to always be right. Unless being right is going to find a cure for a terminal disease, end world hunger or win the lottery for you, does being right always matter. Pick and choose your battles carefully and compromise if necessary. Life is too precious to keep entertaining detractors or confrontational people. Nobody is perfect and there are times that we may have to be the one to apologize or humble ourselves in conflict. It becomes an issue when that is the norm with the same person repeatedly. You can only be the best possible you and hope that others reciprocate. If you find that you are always giving and they are constantly taking, a day may soon come when you have to simply stop and choose yourself first. It may be painful initially to let some people go but nobody ever died from just a broken heart, but doctors have documented that ongoing, unnecessary stress does contribute to serious illnesses and diseases. To make it plain, temporary discomfort may be better for your health long term. Think about and evaluate if your "it" has to do with issues with a person that is consistently adding too much stress to your life. Try to work it out, but it is a two way street. If you have ever flown, you have heard the pilot advise all passengers to put their own mask on first in the event of an emergency. Well, the same concept applies in your life. You can't help anyone until you help yourself first. And there are just some people that you cannot help. You can pick and choose your friends but not your family. Therefore, you will have to take another approach with a parent or other close relatives because they are worth "putting in the work" with. One on one communication without arguing, writing a letter to get all of the issues out or professional counseling depending on the severity of the issue may be necessary for a healthy long term solution or growth. If possible, you should do anything possible or within reason to save or grow your relationships with close relatives. Regardless of which method you take, the answer is never just ignoring it or sweeping the issue under the rug as so many of us are conditioned to do.

Finances

Financial challenges are an ongoing cycle within many family trees. If one starts off in life with an inheritance or a free ride up until their mid-20's, they may have a better financial life than someone who came from a struggling background. Adversely, the opposite can be true for some and we hear about different outcomes often from celebrities, athletes or wealthy people from very humble beginnings. A media contributor to CNN and USA News, Tom Corley, elaborates on this in more depth. For five years, Tom observed and documented the daily activities of 233 wealthy people and 128 people living in poverty. He discovered there is an immense difference between the habits of the wealthy and the poor. During his research he identified over 200 daily activities that separated the "haves" from the "have nots." One of his articles, Breaking the Generational Cycle of Poverty and Reducing Income Inequality, based on his in-depth research explains that 40 percent of all of our daily activities are daily habits. This means 40 percent of the time we are all on auto pilot. If we have good habits, life is good. If we have bad habits, life is bad. Think of a seesaw. On one side of your seesaw are your good habits and on the other side are your bad habits. If you have far more good consistent, financial habits than bad habits you will eventually have a better financial life. If you have far more bad inconsistent, financial habits than good habits you may always have very poor finances. It may sound simple, but a lot of people miss it because their parents did not get it either because of other adversity they may have been trying to survive. It is not intentional, but since we now have more opportunities and know better now, we must do better. We should encourage our families, communities and churches to help change the cycle one step at a time. Within my own church my Pastor, Dr. Reverend William D. Whatley, regularly speaks about and teaches our congregation about saving a percentage from every dollar and other life-changing financial discipline. This is essential because the church is very influential to a large group of people leading families for the next generation. Below are some simple and often overlooked reminders if you are trying to improve your financial status:

1. Spend less than you earn.
2. Stick to a budget.
3. Pay down/off your credit cards.
4. Save regularly even if it is a small amount.
5. Contribute to your 401K (if applicable).
6. Stay out of stores and stop window shopping.

7. Take advantage of points programs at stores and with travel.
8. Go online to find a coupon for everything.
9. Do not ever make a purchase to impress anyone.
10. Have a plan B.

Although you already probably know and practice the 10 tips, repetition helps us to stay on track or improve what we are currently doing right.

Health/Weight Challenges

Our health relates to weight on all levels. This is also another area where most people continue background habits. People that are closer to their ideal weight face less medical issues. Diets are not the answer for everyone but a lifestyle change is for preventative health. According to the Center for Disease Control and Prevention (CDC), research has shown that as people become "overweight" and "obese,"* their risk for developing the following conditions increases:

- Coronary heart disease

- Type 2 diabetes

- Cancers (endometrial, breast, and colon)

- Hypertension (high blood pressure)

- Dyslipidemia (for example, high total cholesterol or high levels of triglycerides)

- Stroke

- Liver and Gallbladder disease

- Sleep apnea and breathing problems

- Osteoarthritis (a breakdown of cartilage and bone within a joint)

- Gynecological problems

*Overweight is defined as a body mass index (BMI) of 25 or higher; obesity is defined as a BMI of 30 or higher.

Well if you are anything like me and most people that I know, you may have a reason to be concerned based on BMI. Even people that eat healthy and exercise regularly struggle with this. It's natural for anyone trying to lose weight to want to lose it very quickly. But evidence shows that people who lose weight gradually and steadily (about 1 to 2 pounds per week) are more successful at keeping weight off. Healthy weight loss isn't just about a "diet" or "program". It's about an ongoing lifestyle that includes long-term changes in daily eating and exercise habits.

To lose weight, you must use up more calories than you take in. Since one pound equals 3,500 calories, you need to reduce your caloric intake by 500−1000 calories per day to lose about 1 to 2 pounds per week. CDC and most nutrition experts advise women to not exceed 2000 calories and men up to 2,800 calories intake per day. Ideally, eating about 1,200 calories (women) – 2,000 calories (men) will help decrease weight by 1-2 pounds weekly if you burn off more than you take in. As you know, losing weight takes more than desire. It takes commitment and a well-thought-out plan. Here's a public online CDC step-by-step guide to getting started.

- Step 1: Make a commitment.
- Step 2: Take stock of where you are.
- Step 3: Set realistic goals.
- Step 4: Identify resources for information and support.
- Step 5: Continually "check in" with yourself to monitor your progress.

The good news is that no matter what your weight loss goal is, even a modest weight loss, such as 5 to 10 percent of your total body weight, is likely to produce health benefits, such as improvements in blood pressure, blood cholesterol, and blood sugars. For example, if you weigh 200 pounds, a 5 percent weight loss equals 10 pounds, bringing your weight down to 190 pounds. While this weight may still be in the "overweight" or "obese" range, this modest weight loss can decrease your risk factors for chronic diseases related to obesity. So even if the overall goal seems large, see it as a journey rather than just a final destination. These habits may help you maintain or lose weight over time. You only have one life to live so live it to the best.

Regardless of where you are on the journey with your personal life, job, career, education and finances, the best is yet to come! We will also explore other areas that your "it" may fall into. Before you expect more, you need to celebrate where you are right now. You may not have the peace, relationship, job, salary, certification or degree that you want yet, but you should still be thankful for your "now". Think back to your anticipation when you completed the application for your current job, apartment, house or signed up for your classes. Back then, you wanted to be accepted and were relieved to find out that you were selected or approved. You may have outgrown where you are, but there was a time when you did not even see beyond where you are right now. You cannot be trusted with more until you are grateful and productive with what you currently have. Be careful to not get caught up with never being content. Take the lessons from your current circumstances as much as possible. It is natural to want more, but do not miss your gifts of the "present". During the journey, you may experience delays or setbacks that make future progress seem unattainable. Always picture yourself beyond your current obstacles because perseverance and faith will help you move forward when the time is right. You may not experience sudden growth or accomplishments when you think it is time, but never give up because your breakthrough could be right around the corner. It would be a shame to give up a few days or months too early. During the most difficult days when you are tempted to throw in the towel, think about how far you have come. Haven't you come too far to turn back now? Can you think back to a time when something worked out when you did not think it would? Even if you cannot think of an example, you will have one soon if you keep moving forward with your action plan that you map out in the following pages. After you make up your mind about what you want to accomplish or overcome, you must make a personal commitment to yourself. You may also feel like you are in a lost place knowing that you do not want to continue in the same job, academic program, relationship, situation or financial state, but you don't know what you prefer or know how to get there. Do not let the uncertainty scare you. Instead, use it to your advantage and explore various options. You may find the perfect fit or solution for yourself if you keep an open mind and think about long term growth. Prepare to change your routine as you privately redefine, reinvest and renew yourself for success or healing. Let your friends and family know briefly that you are working on a project or goal that may require more of your time and that you may not talk to or see them as often for a couple months. Change is uncomfortable for everyone at first. Make a schedule and stick to it. Make up your mind to simplify your life, and do not change it no matter what. Set realistic expectations for yourself because you will be discouraged if you do not experience success right away. Give yourself enough time and options to succeed or overcome obstacles. However, do not set them too low in fear of failure because you should challenge yourself to advance in life. Aim high and you will excel much farther as you pursue your goals and/or dreams. Self-commitment to your plans must be as unmovable as a mountain. You must stand regardless of what storms or heat surrounds your life. You may slow down, be stressed or get discouraged, but never give up. Life is always going to challenge you in some way even if you are not going after your goals or trying to heal. Therefore, giving up on your plans and goals will not make a difference or protect you from stress. If you give up on your plan, you will be even more upset or depressed in the future because you are older and in the same place without growth. *Life is about growth and lessons, but it requires sacrifice, time and work.* If you take care of business now, you will have a better quality of life, joy, education, improved finances or whatever it is that you desire. Do not let temporary discomfort cause you to give up on the big picture or delay your goals or change. Unleash the next level of success or peace within your soul, heart and mind. Depending on your situation or season, it may be time to **redefine** who you are and where you are going.

Chapter 1 Quick Start Take Away

Identify and list prior accomplishments.

Identify and list your "it" or "its".

Identify your fears and challenges.

_____

_____

_____

_____

_____

_____

_____

_____

Chapter 2

What, Why, Who of You

"Are you worth it?"

As you read the previous chapter, you may have found yourself stuck on some of the questions and that is okay. At some point, you may have discovered that you have changed or realized that you are in a completely different place from where you were in the past. **What** you want, need and deserve is mostly within your power. One cannot expect another human to fulfill them regardless of what misleading television shows or your family may have told you. Others can enhance or compliment us. However, our needs and desires are directly connected to self in this Era. Do you want what society, family and friends have conditioned you to want or expect; or is it something that YOU want. At any age, it is very important for us to be clear about this. Going back to something very basic that I think anyone can relate to is that traditionally females have been conditioned to focus on looking good for others' validation, keeping it together so a man will want her, getting married and having children. Whereas males were encourage to be tough, get an education, make money and exceed at sports. Some families send sons to get a college degree while other send their daughters to college to get a MRS degree. The reality is that both genders should have been encouraged to keep themselves up for self, get a good education to create a decent life and define what is important to them as they grow into their life. Many of us have been encouraged or told what to expect based on our gender, race and background. This is not necessarily wrong, but it can limit one's progress or lead them into decisions that really do not fit them.

As you invest yourself more into your what, think about the following:

1. How would accomplishing "what" change my life?

   _____

   _____

   _____

2. Will it make a difference in my life long term?

   _____

   _____

   _____

3. What am I willing to sacrifice?

   _____

   _____

   _____

4. Is it worth it?

   _____

   _____

   _____

Why do you want "it" or exploring a particular change? Will it take you to the next level in any way or give you peace? If so, then how? Since this is about you, there is no right or wrong answer. These questions are just intended to encourage you to stand in your truth....not society, not your family, not your friends, not your organizations truth; but "your" truth. Yesterday way of life does not apply in many scenarios today. In some ways that is good, whereas it is not in others. You are the CEO of your life so execute a plan to live it to the fullest with what you have and where you are. Remember storms and tribulations are a necessary part of life for us all at some point. Unfortunately, some experience downfalls more than others, but you must have "faith" to keep pressing regardless of what the situation is. Depending on the size of your situation, obstacle or truth-----take one day, hour, minute or second at a time.

> *You are the CEO of your life so execute a plan to live it to the fullest with what you have and where you are.*

Regardless of where you are right now, it is never too late to change directions if "your truth" requires it. Often times, we may chose the short term, easier, comfortable, less intimidating, expected or common decisions in life. In some scenarios that may be ideal but in others it may be a long term disaster, dangerous or lead to big regrets. We all know that life will never be perfect, but we do deserve (for the majority of our lives) to be at peace somewhat when we are not putting out fires or dealing with storms in different seasons. As you probably know by now, change is uncomfortable but may be necessary for long term progress.

Two of my own past examples of standing in my own truth and difficult changes that were best for me long-term:

- ❖ In college, one of my parents encouraged me to go to school for nursing because the medical field would provide security. Although I was paying for my own education, to keep the family peace and because I also feared financial failure, I pursued the medical path. My true desire and interest was business, law or psychology. After wasting two years on a path that I did not have passion or any interest in, I changed my entire college plan. Upon researching the three areas that I preferred, I determined Business was best for me to pursue and I completed three degrees up to my MBA. During the degree change, I was very upset and felt like I wasted two years and money, but I knew that I needed to make the change for my "long term" peace and success. People have better success when their career is something they are passionate about. In my case, I started all over and perhaps wasted two years going in the opposite direction to make a relative happy and out of fear of the unknown, but ultimately it was my decision and responsibility. As you could imagine, I was disgusted during the change because I felt like I was never going to finish school. During college, I was also working full time and very active within my family. However, that uncomfortable change was one of the best long decisions I ever made as I am successful and passionate about my career in Business. Throughout the years in various roles, I have earned numerous awards, created revenue driving programs, developed effective processes, overachieved goals and targets because I am "passionate" about business. I doubt if I would have accomplished as much in the medical field because it was not my calling or my passion. We all have different strengths and gifts. Are you in touch with your strengths or gifts? Accepting that I may have wasted a couple of years in the wrong college programs and starting over completely was very frustrating, but it paid off long term for my career and happiness. Sometimes in life, you may have to take a few steps back to win a marathon later.

❖ Another major and more serious decision is when I realized that I had to leave a very unhealthy marriage. That was very difficult because I do not believe in divorce. Although I am divorced today, I still do not believe in it unless there is some type of abuse with no end in sight. Anyone that knew me understood that I was not the typical woman because marriage was not on my life goal list. I was okay with or without it, but most women live for it. Therefore, when I actually fell in love and accepted a proposal from what appeared to be a story book romance, I just knew it would last forever no matter what. Well the problem is that I married the representative and found out about the rest a few years into it. Everyone has different sides and my Ex definitely had a lot of good in him and that is what attracted me to him. However, over the years it became very unhealthy and toxic leaving me no choice but to terminate the marriage. This was the hardest decision I ever had to make in my life because I am not a quitter and failure has never been an option for me. I worried about what would happen to me after I filed for the divorce (but then I became brave and comforted by scripture Isaiah 54:17), what will people think about me having a failed marriage and how do I start life over alone. Regardless of how toxic it became, I learned to deal with it and hide the unacceptable issues for years. One day, I had to stand in my own truth and file papers. It was the healthiest and best long term decision for my situation. There is no perfect marriage and I am always encouraging friends to stay together when they have issues that are not nearly as serious as mine were. My initial self-destructive **what** (don't believe in divorce), **why** (love and didn't want to fail) and **who** (worried about the Ex reaction and family/friends/church perception) definitely delayed my decision longer than necessary, but I eventually had to do what was best. In hindsight, I do not have regrets although it did not work out because I took every precaution as I went in with my eyes open. Since it was a church wedding, we had months of premarital counseling, discussed finances, children, dreams and anything else but it still did not work despite my best efforts. I have never looked back and I have zero regrets.

Whether it is dating, relationships or marriage, sometimes we may **need** something different than what we think we want. A good example would be a particular person you may want to date or marry. Sometimes we can limit ourselves to less than what we deserve. We may see similar patterns growing up, fear being alone or just want the so called American dream. It is important to ask yourself, are you dealing with someone that is quality right now or just potential with passion? Passion is important, but we can end up in the wrong situation later when it is over rated and the sparks fizzle out after health issues, job loss, family issues or something that causes one to not be as "passionate" for a while. Take things at face value-----don't make plans with only "potential". Often times, I hear too many women say they dating a guy they aren't happy with but he has potential. We all are a work in progress, but we should probably operate more on the facts versus the potential. Personally, I have the potential to be the next Venus or Serena Williams, but I am not willing to sacrifice with insane work out, practice and investment on a top tennis coach. My reality is that I exercise four days out of the week for an hour, but my potential is to increase this and be the next star athlete. I think you get the point. In most situations it is better for us to make decisions based on the facts versus the potential. Meanwhile, Mr. Potential can date Ms. Potential and you can date Mr. Fact as you present your fact for a "potentially better outcome". Ponder or plan with what is present. It will save you and the other person time and aggravation when we accept how things truly are. Life is precious and we should not waste too much time trying to force something to fit that may be a mismatch. If it don't fit, don't force it. Of course it is easier said than done, but it is necessary for long term progress and peace.

It's Your Time

Outside of personal relationships, is your **Why** for yourself, family, status, future or a combination? Identifying "why" you are pursuing "what" will help you accomplish or reconsider your goals. Once you figure this out, it will help you strive to the next level because you have purpose behind it. Ask yourself the following:

1. Is my **what** for myself, other people or both?

_____

_____

_____

2. Why should I move forward now or again?

_____

_____

_____

3. Are there any reasons that I should not move forward?

_____

_____

_____

Who are you? Regardless of your age, I think we have all found ourselves re-examining **who** we are as life takes us in various directions. A young adult may have changed due to school and their surroundings. A middle aged adult may have gradually changed due to work, marriage or financial challenges. A more seasoned adult may have gradually changed due to work, marriage, divorce, widow, finances or health issues. Life has a way of forcing us to change intentionally or unintentionally over time. Have you ever been in a situation and asked yourself any of the following questions:

1. How did I get here?

2. Where did the old me go?

3. How did I allow this to happen?

4. How am I going to turn this around?

_____

_____

_____

5. Can I get back to where I use to be?

_____

_____

_____

6. Will I ever get beyond this Season in my life?

_____

_____

_____

If you have asked yourself at least one of those questions, it just confirms that you are human. Actually, it is a good sign because it shows that you want something better. The danger is when we decide to settle completely or give up. Are you exactly who you want to be or do you still think there is room for growth; although, you may already be absolutely fabulous? Often times this will depend on what season you may be in within your own life. Let's take a look at which one you consider yourself to be in right now.

Season is defined in Webster's Dictionary as:

Seasons: *1) Any four divisions of the year; winter, spring, summer and fall. 2) Time when something takes place, is popular, is permitted, etc. 3) The suitable time or period.*

Winter
A period like winter, as the last or final period of life; a period of decline, decay, inertia, dreariness, or <u>adversity</u>.

Spring
To rise or extend upward to come into being by <u>growth</u>, as from a seed or germ, bulb, root, etc.; grow, as plants.

Summer
The period of finest <u>development</u>, perfection, or beauty previous to any decline: sun is out.

Fall
The autumn season is the time of year when the weather <u>transitions</u> from the heat of summer to the cold of winter. Autumn usually lasts from early September to late November. Change colors: orange, brown, gold, etc…

Do you notice that "change" plays a crucial role in all seasons? It takes four seasons to make up the year, just as it takes various seasons to make you who you are. Pay close attention to the seasons' following: adversity, growth, development, transitions. What differentiates you is how you react to your seasons. The seasons in your life positions you closer to the victory of your "it". You cannot make the days on the calendar or situation in your life speed up. In the meantime, you must reposition yourself to get ready to weather the different seasons of change. It's your time to deal with your epiphany and grow to the next level with your goals, internal growth, finances or career.

Among other situations, you may be facing at least one of the following right now:

- Internal void or emptiness
- Emotional baggage
- Health/Weight challenges
- Financial hardship
- Career/Job issues
- Education aspirations or obstacles
- Divorce
- Separation
- Failed personal relationships
- Strained family relationships

There is no book alone that will resolve or eliminate all of the issues on the list. However, inward reflection through this book, resources, time and an "honest effort" from you is the solution for you to overcome or achieve your "it". Time also plays a crucial part of your situation regardless of what your "it" is and nobody has control over time. You only have control over your reaction and what you will do in the meantime during this season. There is a season for everything in life as you evolve, overcome and grow.

Some of your plans may sound easy, but most things are "easier said than done". Do not expect an overnight result or miracle although it is possible. Most people's journey will take time, and the amount of time depends on several factors. It will depend on the goal, situation, circumstance, environment and you. It is important to "start with the end in mind". *What would success or growth be to you in your situation?* Establish that answer to this question early on and focus on it no matter what. Webster's Dictionary defines success as the achievement of something desired, planned, or attempted. Many people automatically think of *success* as wealth or power, but that does not truly define it. Success means something different to everyone depending on circumstances, backgrounds and desires. However, most people want to experience as much success as possible. *What is success to you and why?* Be careful to not measure success based on society, media, friends and family. Some of the following questions may apply to you or someone that you care about. *Is it time for a change in your life? What season are you in right now? Are you putting off something you have desired to do for you for awhile? Do you worry about your future? Are you tired of worrying about money? Do you want to grow to your fullest potential? Are you surrounded by people who help or hurt you? Do you want to continue your education? Are you still trying to figure out your purpose here? Do you want a better job? Are you dealing with negative family or friends? Are you having issues with people you repeatedly try to help and forgive? Do you feel alone and discouraged? Do you need to increase or find peace and joy? Do you often doubt if you really can do it or make it? Do you feel like you are at the end of the rope? Have you ever thought that you may be better off not here? Are you afraid? Are you tired? Are you sick and tired of being sick and tired?* **Hold on anyway!** You can and will make it regardless of your "it" if you have a plan and follow it!

Chapter 2 Quick Start Take Away

Identify your what *(may be multiple)*.

Identify your why *(may be multiple)*.

Identify your who *(may be multiple)*.

_____

_____

_____

_____

_____

_____

_____

_____

_____

_____

Redefine, Reinvest, Renew

Chapter 3

What Do You Really Want or Need Next?

"Are you staying in your lane?"

Ensure that what you want lines up with what you need. Nobody can tell you what you need or want. You will evaluate and determine this with your realistic viewpoint as you work on the questions that only you can truly answer. And if it does not, work it out with yourself before making a mistake you may have to clean up later. We have all heard the old saying, "Going in with your eyes open." Somehow, some of us may still see what we want to see although it is not reality. That my sister, is what I refer to as daydreaming denial. In some instances, some daydreaming is healthy when it comes to achieving goals that are within in our control (i.e.-education, home buying, financial targets, starting a business or paying off debts) and healthy as we have a vision. Tangible daydreaming is quite healthy when it leads you to take action with a plan and necessary research. However, daydreaming denial which is not healthy are those scenarios when we think Mr Obvious Wrong will somehow be Mr. Right; although, his Joker cards are on the table, assume a dead end job will miraculously turn into a dream job without doing the work, or a very dysfunctional family will suddenly become the The Waltons, Brady Bunch or Fresh Prince. In most situations, it is what it is regardless of what we prefer. While some situations are not within our control, our reaction and responses are.

Often times we confuse what we may **want** with a **need**. Our needs usually require less effort than a want, but it is helpful to identify which category it falls within. This is important because it will help you prioritize, plan and have more of a realistic approach. Regardless of whether it is a need or want, you can accomplish it with a realistic plan, and sacrifice just as you have in other areas of your life. Do you feel like you want or need a change in a stagnant or unfulfilling job, home or is it an inside job? How long have you been feeling this way? Do you see things getting worse or better?

Needs and wants are not always something related to money, status or material gain. You may have internal growth to accept, goals, to overcome life changes or storms. External goals are easier to evaluate and more noticeable (*i.e.-material gain, weight loss, job change*). Internal goals may be difficult to evaluate (*i.e.- healing, peace, forgiveness*) because there are different phases of the process. Therefore it is essential to write everything down on your quest to success or overcoming obstacles. Initially, it will be difficult to remember to write and revisit your notes. With consistency, it will become a routine that you look forward to. Some may say it becomes a discipline or a self-checkpoint to keep you focused despite the pressures of everyday life and responsibilities. Regardless of whether you are facing goals related to healing, education, career, relationship or internal growth; the following steps will assist you on the journey.

Many concepts, systems and methods are available to guide your goal setting. One of the most common, simple and straightforward goal setting methods is SMART.

S = Specific
Be clear about what you want to overcome or achieve.

M = Measurable
Identify criteria for measuring progress toward the goal attainment.

A = Attainable
Set goals that are possible so that you remain motivated.

R = Realistic
Set goals that you can attain in reasonable time with honest effort.

T = Timely
Time must be realistic, measurable and attainable.

If you do not write your new goals down, you have already failed. Life is too busy to carry it around in your head. You will also lose ideas and dreams if you don't maintain written goals and track your progress.

Build onto your goals beyond this book journey. Make sure you complete the questions within this book journey as you jumpstart or reignite your dream, goal or resolution. You may want to even elaborate more and keep an additional journal for long term goals that require additional space and focus. Regardless of what method or routine you use, with any serious pursuit of goals, you must ensure that it is measurable, attainable, realistic and timely.

Step 1 – List Specific Goals

Goals with realistic expectations are attainable. Many people get overwhelmed when they state everything that they want to achieve because of the sacrifices and personal requirements. Anything internal or external worth having requires change that may be uncomfortable initially. You must know what you want before you can achieve it. Just saying that you want more out of life is too vague. You need to be more specific about exactly what you want, and why you want it. Do not find yourself disappointed if you do not get exactly or close to what you want because you never stated it. Don't aimlessly wander through life without a clear purpose or goal beyond just work and paying bills. What is your goal? Is it inner peace, healing, joy, degree, house, auto, a mate, a companion, to minimize debt or something else that you have been pursuing for awhile? State what your specific goals are.

_____

_____

_____

_____

_____

_____

Redefine, Reinvest, Renew

Step 2 - Define Goal

Defining your goals will help you along your journey. You must know exactly what you are working towards in order to stay focused during the chaos of life and other obligations. Working, paying bills and the unexpected can be demanding and overwhelming. It is easy to get off track if you do not define your goals and set a timeline. Define the type of degree, type of house, type of car you can afford, qualities expected in relationships, depth of pain to recover from, how much debt you want to pay off and by when. Be very specific when you are defining goals.

_____

_____

_____

_____

_____

_____

_____

_____

Redefine, Reinvest, Renew

Step 3 - Set Timeline

You must set a timeline in order to succeed. Set a realistic timeline to achieve your goals so that you will not lose interest or motivation. It may take you longer to accomplish your goal (i.e.-weight loss, gaining internal joy, peace, better job, a degree or house) but the quantity of time is not important. Reaching your goal within a realistic timeline that works around your current responsibilities is important. Your health, immediate family, and income are first and foremost. You can accomplish anything that you set out to accomplish! Flexible weekday and weekend classes, online classes, job training, home buying programs, and any other life improvement options exist everywhere you turn. There is no excuse to not accomplish your goal if you truly want to. The internet and local library contains a wealth of information. Find what will work with your life demands and set a timeline right now. Stop waiting and set a specific personalized timeline.

_____

_____

_____

_____

_____

_____

Redefine, Reinvest, Renew

Step 4 - Plan and Strategize

Another crucial formula to success is planning! In order to succeed, you must plan and come up with a strategy. Write down your current schedule and responsibilities. Make a list of the areas in your life that are flexible and that are not. For example, you can minimize (not stop) family/friend visits, optional organizations, email and phone time. You, your household, spirituality and income are the vital areas that should not be sacrificed. I am not advocating kicking your extended family and friends to the curb completely. However, you may need to take a step back from some of them for a short period of time in order to pursue your goals more aggressively.

_____

_____

_____

_____

_____

_____

_____

Redefine, Reinvest, Renew

Step 5 - Time Management

Remain focused and motivated about your goals. You will have more time to do the things you are sacrificing later. You may even be in a relationship that changes because of it, but stay focused regardless. If someone really cares about you, they will be supportive. Believe it or not, you may run into a situation with an insecure companion that threatens to end the relationship if you spend a little less time with him/her and go back to school sacrificing just a few hours a week or for other self-growth. The best decision you can make for you both (if you are not married) is to show him/her the door because a companion like that is baggage and dead weight holding you back. On your journey, you may have to sacrifice non-marital relationships, fun, sleep, dates and invitations that may fall on the same days as classes or other obligations. Regardless, stay focused on what will get you closer to what is best for you. Some people may say that you are being extreme, going too far or changing too much. That is okay because you are changing for the better for yourself. You cannot focus on pleasing all people (relatives, friends, co-workers) around you and be how you use to be. Growth is change. Anything worth having takes sacrifice, change and growth. You cannot get something for nothing.

Time management will be your ongoing challenge from the start until the end. You may have long term goals such as working toward a certification, a degree or saving for a house. During the journey towards the goal, you will be faced with unexpected events. You cannot allow these unexpected life events to take over long term or you will find yourself off track completely. However, some life events *(i.e.-moving, changing jobs, relative's sickness or death)* may definitely require you to drastically revise your schedule. Time management is crucial throughout your entire journey. As stated earlier in previous chapters, beware of negative people and environments. If someone is telling you to take a break or anything to insinuate that you should put your goals off; distance yourself from that person and reflect on your goal and the future benefits. Some people are uncomfortable with your growth because it highlights their lack of growth or achievements. Also, please do not allow people to waste your time with gossip and drama. List and organize all of your time effectively on paper. You may not be able to follow the schedule perfectly, but it will be a good weekly guide for you.

_____

_____

_____

_____

_____

_____

It's Your Time

List your schedule and analyze how you spend your time.

	Morning	Afternoon	Evening
Sunday			
Monday			
Tuesday			
Wednesday			
Thursday			
Friday			
Saturday			

Step 6 - Action Plan

Time and energy is scarce as you already know. You may discover that you have to shift things around a few times until you find what works for your current schedule. Additional time may be discovered when you decrease phone calls, emails, addictive social media and other optional daily time-consuming routines. In order for this to work, you need to follow your schedule like a sick person follows a medical prescription. It will not be easy and comfortable initially, but it will be worth it! Remember to let your close friends and family know that you will not be able to talk or see them as often while you work on areas to improve your life. You do not need to go into the details with everyone. Some people may unintentionally give you negative energy that you do not need. Tell people just enough so that they know you are not upset with them, but you're busy pursuing a personal goal. Keep your eyes and mind set on your goal. Follow your outlined daily schedule as close as possible. Sometimes unexpected things may come up to throw you off track for a day or a week, but do not get discouraged. Just get back on track and keep working towards your goal. For example, you may be saving for a house but your car may have an expensive repair. Do what you have to do to repair it or trade it in, but do not give up on your goal for that house although the car issue or some other financial detour may have set you a few months back from your original goal. Other common life detour examples: your job may cause you to work overtime, your child may be sick, severe relationship issues emerge, loss of a loved one or anything unexpected that throws you off of your path. Naturally, these detours may throw you off from studying and classes; but keep your head up and get back on track after you do what you have to do. Do not give up when obstacles and unexpected issues keep arising. You need to handle the issue to the best of your ability and keep following your plan. It may even take you longer than planned, but that is okay. Keep on, keepin' on no matter what! Later is better than never. If you haven't discovered it yet, you will notice more and more unexpected life detours the closer you get to your goal or internal growth. Therefore, you should do yourself a favor and anticipate detours along the way. When possible, have a plan B ready.

_____

_____

_____

_____

_____

_____

_____

_____

_____

As you work towards your plan, make sure that you are being truthful to yourself about the plan based on your schedule, obligations and daily demands. Even if it may take you a little longer to achieve your "it", all that matters is that you will accomplish it in due time. Do not compare yourself to other people even if your circumstances are similar. You will never be at peace or remain focused if you compare your progress with someone else. Furthermore, make sure that you associate yourself mostly with people that have the same interests or values. It is still good to have some various associations to keep a grip on reality outside of just your interests and strive to be well rounded.

> *You will never be at peace or remain focused if you compare your progress with someone else.*

If you are having a difficult time deciding what you need versus want right now, that is fine. Sometimes a real, life-changing decision takes time but if you continue to seek, you will find. Do not rush your process and jump into something that may cause you to regress or further confusion. Think back to your original life plans, dreams and goals. As many, you probably are living a completely different reality, but you can still use your inner strengths and passions within your current life. Perhaps, you wanted to be the next Patti LaBelle, Nora Jones, John Legend or Beyonce but you don't quite see that happening now; you can still use your voice gift to sing at city local events, weddings, nursing home programs and choirs. You can still get fulfillment by using your gift, make extra income and uplift groups of people within your own community. Before you know it, you could be a local hometown star. Make the best with what you have where you are right now. Success is not only wealth and fame.

Sometimes it is simply fulfillment and peace. Have you ever heard the saying, "More money, more problems"? Look at the controversy and early deaths of some major, rich icons. Be careful what you ask for. It costs to be the boss.

Chapter 3 Quick Start Take Away

Identify your need(s).

Identify your want(s).

Identify what you are willing to sacrifice.

_____

_____

_____

_____

_____

_____

_____

_____

_____

Redefine, Reinvest, Renew

Chapter 4

Redefine Based on Your Reality

"Are you still living in yesterday?"

Throughout some of life defeats, losses and tragedies, you probably learned many lessons along the way. Perhaps, you may still be learning right now. I personally learned the most from loss, heartbreak, discrimination, financial challenges or other dark situations. As I recovered, healed and prospered; I realized that sometimes you have to lose in order to win. In some situations, it makes sense to just "surrender" and be better off in the long run. What may be perceived as failure when something does not work out is actually a sign that you may need to go a different direction or do something else. However, in some situations, failure is not an option. It is up to you to figure out when to surrender and when to battle as if you are fighting for your life. As long as there is breathe in your body, you can redefine, reinvest and renew yourself. I trust that since you are reading this page, there is breathe in your body. So let's do it. Depending on your situation or goal, it may not be as drastic as you think. You may be able to work it into your weekly routine without as much sacrifice as you dread. Make it a priority as you deprioritize some things. If you work in one hour every day for yourself the "majority" of the week (i.e. - 5 days), that is at least 5 hours/20 hours a month/260 hours a year for YOU. Use that time exclusively for yourself.

Redefine is to reexamine or reevaluate especially with a view after change or to transform yourself. Do not let others define you. Who are you today regardless of yesterday (marriage, separation, divorce, loss, financial problems, dysfunctional family or embarrassing situations). Your reaction to adversity will determine who you are. Some examples of dynamic icons who redefined themselves after a momentary defeat is Nelson Mandela *(late anti-apartheid revolutionary, politician and philanthropist who served as President of South Africa)*, **Russell Herman** *(late founder and CEO of Herman J. Russell and Company, national entrepreneur and succeed at many projects which included Hartsfield-Jackson Atlanta International Airport, GA Dome, Phillips Arena, and Turner Field)*, **Vanessa Williams** *(Singer, Actress, Producer, and was the first African-American crowned Miss America)* and **Iyanla Vanzant** *(Inspirational Speaker, Lawyer, Author, Life Coach and Television Personality)*. Mandela was imprisoned for standing up for justice, but he overcame what was meant to kill his spirit and destroy him. Instead of letting prison define him, he came out stronger than ever and served as the President over the same biter government that imprisoned him. Herman faced bitter racism as one of the first minorities buying property in Georgia. Instead of allowing racists to hold him back and define him, he went around them by hiring a Caucasian man to buy the property for him and then transferred it to Herman. He went around the evil, racist, success blockers right under their ignorant noses. In Williams' situation, an old nude picture surfaced after she won and then the first minority Miss America was dethroned. During her time as Miss America, she received death threats and had more security than any predecessor. Toxic haters were determined to find something to take her down and they did temporarily. However, she did not allow the humiliation from being dethroned end her success. Instead she made a well-received and successful comeback in music and television. Vanzant faced several defeats also, but she bounced back from a career changing fall out with Oprah (which is now repaired) and Barbara Walters, which lead to failed shows. She did not give up and allow the very public situation to define her. She

redefined her fate and success by not allowing the negative press and haters defeat her as many celebrities have. Now Vanzant has three successful shows and more due to her tenacity. Do not allow anyone or situation to write your story. Learn from whatever comes your way and rise above it, sail through it or bust is wide open.

As you face the seasons in your life, you may have an epiphany. Often times an epiphany brings about a desire or requirement for major shift and life changing decisions.

According to Webster's Dictionary, **Epiphany** is defined as:

A comprehension or perception of reality by means of a sudden intuitive realization.

A sudden manifestation of the essence or meaning of something.

A sudden, intuitive perception of or insight into the reality or essential meaning of something, usually initiated by an occurrence or experience.

In other words, an epiphany is a strong wake up call or realization. You may have already experienced an epiphany about your situation, but it may be too difficult to face or easier to just ignore it. If you are browsing this page, you are probably ready or overdue for a positive change, motivated, disappointed, hurt and/or tired. Regardless of the page you are on within your own life, it demands "action" from you. Face your epiphany because you are the only one who can do anything about it. It is never too late regardless of your age, economic status, education level, gender, background or situation. If it was too late, you would not be reading this page right now. Physical death is the only circumstance that is "too late" for you to get through or past where you are right now. Since you are reading this page, it obviously is not too late for you to accomplish your goals, change, grow, find peace and/or resolve issues in your life. As you know by now, life is complex and unpredictable regardless of how much you give, how hard you work, sacrifice, forgive, try to forget, take the high road, turn the other cheek, get up after getting knocked down by circumstances repeatedly, situations and/or people. Before you know it, you may find yourself in a routine or cycle of just existing, but not living or feeling anymore. Your "journey" in this book is all about what you want it to be and provides essential tools that you need to get up, through and over where you are now. Be real with yourself as you read, meditate, answer questions and work on your journal questions in this book. For the record, please understand that nothing in this book is intended to be unrealistic and inconsiderate by saying, just get over it. People say "just get over it" all of the time but it usually is not that simple. Often times, most people are lying to themselves and eventually figure out that they are delaying a problem or situation when they believe they can simply get over or achieve "it" quickly just because they say the words. In due time, you will accomplish whatever you need to with faith, patience, perseverance, and determination. Things may not always turn out how you think you prefer or desire, but the key is what's best for you and anyone that you are responsible for. The outcome may not be what you want although it may be exactly what you need!

Redefine, Reinvest, Renew

Take an honest and transparent look at where you are:

1. What situation/incident have you been set back by?

_____

_____

_____

_____

_____

_____

2. How did it affect you overall?

_____

_____

_____

_____

_____

_____

3. Are you still dealing with haters? How and why?

_____

_____

_____

_____

_____

_____

4. What are you going to do to get past the setback?

_____

_____

_____

_____

_____

_____

5. What epiphany did you have from this situation?

_____

_____

_____

_____

_____

_____

If you are defining your career, business, education or dealing with a personal goals, you may have a much easier path than someone recovering and redefining their life due to a major life event like death, divorce, home fire, auto

accident or job loss. At the time of the storm, pain, loss, shock, drama, tragedy or disappointment, we may be convinced that we will never be able to recover. Some people take longer than others because they may have different circumstances and backgrounds. Although timing may vary, everyone can recover from almost anything as long as they get up every day. Sometimes just getting up out of the bed to face another day carrying the weight of the "it" seems impossible, but just take one day at a time. I know this first hand from prior tragedies and storms in my own life. Back then, I heard my alarm clock go off repeatedly, but I could not get up; although, I knew I would be late for work. It took so much out of me just to get my feet on the floor to start my day when I felt like I was going through hell. I wanted to stay in bed to sleep so that I would not have to feel the pain burn in my heart, stomach, have stress headaches, cry and face my fears concerning my situations. Can you relate? It was so overwhelming at times that I locked most people out, lost a lot of hair and short term memory daily. When I say just getting my feet on the floor next to my bed was a struggle, I literally mean just that. I felt like giving up several times. But even in the lowest valleys, I did get up eventually and you can too. My late grandfather, Herbert Lee Williams, use to always encourage people by saying, "Take just one day at a time," very often but I did not understand that phrase when I was a child, but I do now. I actually say, "Take one hour at a time," because life can quickly get overwhelming. Often times, people defeat themselves within their own heads by trying to take on too much at once. Have you ever made up your mind to do something, but changed your mind after you thought about everything that could go wrong? Did you ever stop to think about everything that could go right? Did you think about how you would feel if you at least gave it an honest try? If you stop and truly think about it, you are probably dealing with the same situation from years or months ago. Why? Are you afraid? What or who are you afraid of? The "unknown" is the most common fear among everyone regardless of age, background or the issue. One of my favorite Oprah Winfrey quotes in <u>What I know for Sure</u>, "Your journey begins with a choice to get up, step out, and live fully."

One way to face your fear of the "unknown" is to think about how long this lingered, how it may have become even worse as you delayed action, accept that it will not disappear and it may even become toxic.

We all hear the common saying, "Life is too short," all of the time but are you living and managing your life as if you truly know that. None of us know when our last day will be, but we do owe it to ourselves to live the best quality of life within our control. Are you managing your life or is life managing you? If you had to think about that question too long, life is probably managing you. Life manages most people because so many events happen beyond our control regardless of how much love, work, time, attention

> *It is uncomfortable to step out of your comfort zone; it is required if you intend to move forward or up.*

and money may be invested. Most people operate on the defense due to the fear of more unexpected situations such as: job loss, divorce, separation, bankruptcy, foreclosure, death of loved ones, deception and other life changing events. Naturally, you would be on the defense after getting knocked down emotionally, financially, psychologically and/or spiritually. Defense must be followed by offense in order to stay in the game of life. You will never see a basketball, football or baseball game without both. And let's face it, life is like a game! You lose some and you win some, but make sure that you bring your "A" game. Even if you strike or foul out, you can find peace or have a sense of pride within yourself when you know that you gave your best. You may realize that you did not give your best, but at least you learned something from it. The lesson should keep you from repeating it again if you really learned from it. The ugly reality is that some of us are dealing with the same situations or unachieved goals because we keep making the same choices or not making a choice although the writing may be on the wall. Do not allow yourself to be by definition,

74

insane. The definition of "insanity" is repeating the same actions, getting the same results but expecting a different outcome. Another old saying by an unknown author is, "You must do something you have never done before to get something or achieve something you never had." It is uncomfortable to step out of your comfort zone, but it is required if you intend to move forward or up in your personal, professional, financial and/or spiritual life. However, you need to acknowledge what you do have and where you are, and be thankful and content first. You may say that you do not have anything to be content about. Well, I do not know your situation but I can tell you that you should be content and thankful for having your right mind as you decided to read this book for growth. Your mind is nothing to take for granted because there are many people that are not in their right mind! Trust me, I lived through some scary situations and saw that first hand. It is a priceless blessing to even be in "your" right mind when you deal with others who may not be. By now, you have probably discovered that we live among many people in this world who are not all operating in their right mind. In that scenario, it is nearly impossible to make progress or resolve the issue and eventually you may be distracted or discouraged.

Even if you have demanding daily distractions and obligations, you can still redefine, reinvest in or renew yourself if you truly "commit to yourself". Often times, we do so much for others at work and home, but it is time to make a commitment to yourself, and stick to it. If you do not, you may reach a point where you will not be able to or want to be there for everyone else anymore. Be proactive and get on offense starting now. "Team Me" may sound selfish but it is not, it is simply *self-preservation*. Once you take care of yourself, then you can help others even more. You cannot help anyone else until you help yourself! And you may even realize that after you help yourself, you cannot help someone else who does not "consistently do what they need to do" to help themselves. Again, life is too short and do not allow yourself to be classified as insane. We have all been there a time or so, but do not take a permanent residence at the insanity subdivision. There are too many residents already there. Don't you deserve to live in a much better and healthier place internally? It may be a hard truth to accept but as you grow, you may have to leave some people, places and comfortable habits behind. It may be a challenge, painful and uncomfortable but it may be necessary. You may have to wake up earlier, go to bed later, sacrifice and distance yourself from some relatives or friends. Keep your eye on the prize or unwavering peace. Regardless of whether the prize is healing, peace, a degree, financial recovery, new job, transportation, home or a new dream, keep your eye on the light at the end of the tunnel. Some tunnels may be longer than others. Most of the time, the bigger pay off comes after one struggles through a long tunnel. Do you want to be ready to win the game, get through the tunnel, and stay out of the insanity subdivision? Some of the questions below will help you as you evaluate your situation. Please keep in mind that no right, wrong, good or bad answers exist because this is all about "you" being true to yourself, your situation and your future.

Chapter 4 Quick Start Take Away

Identify what changed, ended or expired in your life.

Identify how it affects you and your daily life.

Identify how you will reposition and overcome.

_____

_____

_____

_____

_____

_____

_____

_____

_____

_____

_____

Redefine, Reinvest, Renew

_____

_____

_____

_____

_____

_____

_____

_____

_____

_____

_____

_____

_____

_____

_____

Chapter 5

Control Your Controllables

"Are your expectations realistic?"

The reality about life is that we do not have much control over most things that affect us daily, but we can control our mind, responses, our diet, household budget, time management, our education and career choices somewhat. Your energy should be vested in what you can control, influence or improve. Do not waste time or energy obsessing over things you cannot control. Also, make sure you are not enabling people around you to waste your time with their negativity about things that are not within their control. Misery loves company. Feed your interest with

> *Continue to teach people how to treat you in every area of your life.*

workshops, seminars, local events, books or any forward moving subject matters that interest you. Surround yourself with people that are headed or already in the same place. Control what you can control. No matter how nice or giving you are, you can't control anyone. Accept who people are and what they say. Do not appease yourself with what you think they meant to say or do. If that was the case, they would have said or done so. Decide what you will and will not accept. Continue to teach people how to treat you in every area of your life including work, school, community and personal. Some people may not like you for whatever reason although you did not do anything to them. Do not allow someone else's problem with you, to become a problem for you. Stop being who you think people want you to be because you will stay or be unhappy long term if you are not yourself the majority of the time. Now of course we cannot just let anything fly out of our mouth and do whatever the heck we want without consequences or potentially making it worse. If we choose success, we all have to still put a certain face on for work, school, events and other public places.

However, do not compromise who you are or settle for lack of integrity or respect. You should re-channel energy from getting overwhelmed about some situations that are beyond our control. There is a lot that we cannot control when it comes to our loved ones, friends, jobs and life overall. However, let's take a look at a few examples on controllable areas within life:

Family/Relationships/Friendships

- Play your position even when you do not feel like it. You go to work plenty of days that you do not feel like it, so why give less to your loved ones.

- Remain positive even when you face adversity. Negativity will only make a bad situation worse.

- Be careful and act based on long-term more than you react in the moment. Short term wrong decisions can destroy long term life progress.

- Protect your brand, image and aspirations by aligning yourself with what you stand for and where you aspire to go. Water and oil don't mix.

- Decrease or eliminate spending time with chronically negative people because it is contagious. If you can't find any positive people in your current circle, be alone and look into positive, relevant workshops, seminars and community organizations.

Work

- Periodically check yourself to ensure that you are exceeding your job requirements. Never get comfortable regardless of how secure you feel or what your title is.

- Be proactive in knowing the overall health of your company, the company's mission/goals/objectives and how your role fits into the puzzle. Play your position and demonstrate your value. Get yours!

- Beyond financial compensation, identify your growth from your job and what you want short and long-term. Take advantage of training programs, workshops or tuition reimbursement for your own personal growth and position yourself to be more marketable.

- Control and protect your brand. You may not get along with some people who may be kiss ups, gossipers, company spies, needy for a friend, nosy or kept to themselves. Actually it is safer to keep a distance with most people while still being a team player. It is safer to be seen as a performing individual instead of being associated with any particular clichés because you do not need to risk other people's brand being placed on you especially if it is not positive. It is also healthy to venture out to know what other departments are doing and introduce yourself.

- During your dreadful commute to and from work (via car, train, bus or by foot), enjoy music, read something empowering or talk to positive people to avoid letting the commute stress you out.

Environment

- Home (House, Apt, Room)
Your home is your sanctuary. It does not matter if you own a mansion, average size home, apartment or rent a room. Wherever you call home, it should be soothing and peaceful with your style. You may not have the budget or time right now to have everything perfect but you can do some basics to make it feel like home. Bring out the best in your house, apartment or room with picture collages of happy memories of key people in your life, favorite color vases, plants, inspirational trinkets, wall borders or fresh paint to bring your space to positive life. Many people procrastinate waiting to have time to make big changes, but start with just one or two small changes. You will feel the difference in your sanctuary.

- Job (Office, Cube or Desk)
  - Work is out of our control to a certain extent but even the smallest customization can make your second home feel more like your zone. Make it your own whether you have a high rise corner office, average size office

without windows, cubical or just a desk. I have heard many people say they don't personalize their work space because they do not plan on staying or they want to make it easy to leave if their position is eliminated. They do have a good point but it may be better to live in the present and make the best of your second home until a change happens. The change may not take place until six months or six years from now. You don't have to invest a lot of money or bring personal pictures in if you are private. However, you can make it yours with a plant, vase, pictures with inspirational phrases, your favorite quotes, photographs of a favorite destination or past trip to inspire you for the next one. Have something positive, pleasant or uplifting in the space where you spend hours daily.

Finances

Your income may not be where it needs to but you can continue "making the most of what you have" with some changes or free tools to help you progress. I'm not personally a financial advisor but I will share some of my financial mentors that I listened to and free resources that I used to control my finances wherever possible. It takes time and you should be patient with yourself. Use the resources available to you to make the most of what you do have until you make your desired income. There are proven and affordable tools out there to help you to help yourself if you are serious about taking charge, moving out of your comfort zone and ready to make some sacrifices. An example of a free online tool that was helpful to me is Suzie Orman's (Author, Financial Advisor, Motivational Speaker, and Television Host) Debt Eliminator and Debt Tracker (www.suzeorman.com/suze-tools/debt-eliminator). It is interactive with real time advice and other areas of advice, tools and resources.

- Get free money on the table with 401K match plans or similar plans with your employer even if you feel like you cannot afford it. If you are waiting on a better time, know that it never comes. Do not leave free money on the table. It may be the only way to save consistently with the bonus of your company match. Areas beyond simple 401K may seem intimidating or difficult to understand if it is new to you. Initially it was for me too, but I discovered many resources like Forbes, Fortune, Black Enterprise and interactive talk radio/website Clark Howard Show. The Clark Howard show is very beneficial because it advises consumers on ways to save more, spend less, and avoid rip-offs. It also provided me with easy to understand insight on IRA, mutual funds and other investments. From there, I gained more insight from NAIC and Vanguard. I encourage you to leverage none commission based financial advisors for your benefit as you increase your knowledge on whatever you may be interested in or curious about.

- Consider increasing your monthly cash and decrease payments on auto, renters, medical and homeowners insurance (if possible). Most people choose smaller deductible fearing paying a $1000 instead of $500 deductibles. In reality, most people do not have to file a claim for years or never. The money that you save monthly with lower payments can help you be in a better cash flow position if you do ever have to file a claim eventually. Make as much of your money as possible work for you now.

- If you have children, you can save more money in the long run with Season or Frequent Visitor Passes to places that you visit on a regular basis (at least 3 times a year). It may be a large sacrifice on the front end but you would end up saving a lot more later. Some examples where I saved a lot of money with Season passes and/or other discounts were Auto Club AAA, Stone Mountain Park, Six Flags and American Adventure. Years ago, I was definitely scrapping paycheck to paycheck with more going out than coming in so I saved money with AAA recreation services, Stone Mountain Park unlimited passes, restaurant and theme park coupons. Also be sure to check out current issues of magazines or websites like Parents, Family Circle and Working Mother for other fun and saving tips.

On a regular basis, I was always growing and finding ways to make $1 stretch to $5. Like you, some of the changes are just cutting down on utilities and changing rate plans after observing my own household patterns and couponing. Other areas of my financial progress came from realistic budgeting, and tips from Money Matter type articles from Alfred Edmond Jr (SVP/Editor-at-large of Black Enterprise, host of Money Matters and Urban Business Roundtable), AAA membership savings, Howard and Orman. One or two changes in how you think about and manage money consistently does make a difference long term. If you are anything like I was before my financial breakthrough, you may have had more bills and overhead than the income coming in. In that situation, you may not think you can save even $5-$50 per pay period but you can with creative bill payments. For example, if my utility bill was $130, I paid $100 to free up $30 for savings and applied this same concept to any other bills besides my mortgage and car note. By the time I shaved off money from each flexible bill, I began to slowly accumulate an emergency fund. Rent, mortgage and car notes are not flexible. Every other bill will work with you as long as you communicate with them. In our economy, you have to work with what you have and stop waiting for an unrealistic, financial miracle. No matter how financially stretched you are, you have to squeeze something out to save even if you start with just $5. You have to make it happen because nobody else will.

In your life right now, let's explore and examine what is within your control right now.

1. How is your mindset?

   _____

   _____

   _____

2. What are you doing and feeling about future success?

   _____

   _____

   _____

3. How is your home environment, and how will you make it even more positive?

   _____

   _____

   _____

4. How is your workspace, and are changes needed?

   _____

   _____

   _____

5. How do you make the most of your work commute?

   _____

   _____

   _____

The same is true for just about every other area of your life. You are the architect to build, shape, mold or demolish the majority of what happens or does not happen. Some people are just driven and progressive naturally. Others may be drifters that do not take charge of controllable(s) unless a life event or emergency occurs. Drifters may not like how some areas of their life currently is but they just go with the flow because that's all they have ever seen growing up, are unmotivated or it could be fear. Fear defeats people every day and is an overlooked success and peace blocker. Fear is a distressing emotion aroused by impeding danger, evil, pain or change. Just like stress, some fear is healthy because it may force necessary progress, movement or change under pressure. Adversely, if not channeled properly, fear can be paralyzing and keep you in a pit of failure or distress. Remember, the fact is that everything about your life beyond your Maker, starts and ends with you. Even if unfair background or situations have made life more difficult than it should be for you, it is time to work on controlling everything that you can to get on a new page. Try to get beyond blaming others for your justifiable anger towards other people that may have let you down or deceived you. Those crabs have probably moved on to disrupting the next person's life. You owe it to yourself to cut their draining and disruptive energy from your life and thoughts. It is time to rebuild, restore, learn, grow beyond fear and control what you can forward.

Chapter 5 Quick Start Take Away

Identify what and who you do not have control of.

Identify solutions to deal with difficult situations.

Identify what is in your control.

_____

_____

_____

_____

_____

_____

_____

_____

_____

_____

It's Your Time

Chapter 6

*Create Your Happy
Even in a Storm*

"Are you investing your energy wisely?"

How much joy or happiness do you consistently have in your life? Are you living or just existing? Even if you are happy, do you desire more? What is your definition of happy or joy? Do you depend solely on exterior things for joy? Is it all internal for you or a combination of both? As you have probably discovered by now, exterior based happiness does not provide long term joy. If you are anything like I was long ago, you probably were waiting "until a situation or person in your life was better" before you did things to make yourself happy. Without realizing it, your happiness is probably contingent on something outside of yourself. That will put you in a position to wait forever because something will always be going on in life and timing is not always the best the majority of the time. Get beyond waiting for your happiness and learn how to even create your happy during the storm. Material things and people can "enhance" whatever happiness we have but it should never be the sole factor. Don't get me wrong, I know that a Coach, Louis Vuitton, Prada, Gucci, Versace, Kate Spade, Michael Kors purse, jewelry or shoes will bring a smile to your face if someone dropped it on you as a gift. However, true and long term joy must come from within. Although we know this, we may get off track and get distracted in the game of life. Have you ever let someone steal your joy without you even realizing how they may have gotten under your skin or on your last reserved nerve? Have you ever allowed your day to be ruined over something or someone insignificant? Have you ever lost sleep over family or friend drama? I have definitely been guilty of all three above before my epiphany. A few times throughout my life, I made certain decisions based on what I thought would make others happy, respect me or include me. The problem is that I wasn't really content or happy with it. Sometimes, I was living my life for other people instead of myself. If you are being completely honest with yourself, at one time you did too. An ideal and drastic example of this is also Elizabeth Gilbert's life story in Eat, Pray and Love. Her whole life was a lie until she walked away from the storybook perfect life at age 30. When I heard Elizabeth speak at a conference, one thing that she said that really stuck with me was, "I stopped being who I was to be who I needed to be." Thank goodness, my situation was not as drastic and yours probably isn't either. To a certain extent, parents and spouses are required to sacrifice drastically to coexist. Don't get too busy for yourself and lose touch with simple activities or routines that make you happy or give you a lift. You do not have to spend money to find your happy center or escape for a few minutes or couple hours each week. What simple routine or hobby makes you feel better or give you a lift? Are you stuck right here trying to think of something or remember if you ever really had a hobby. You may not even know because you may be so focused on what makes your family and friends happy for so long. You may draw a long blank when you try to focus on yourself. You have to change that and get back in touch with yourself. Be patient with yourself and don't expect a major breakthrough overnight. I have been in this place too and a technique that was helpful was time management, making and consistently working a list. Eventually, I came up with my list and will list some of my own examples of ideas for you just in case you also can't think of something simple and uplifting for yourself. Put yourself on your calendar as if it is a meeting or doctor's appointment that you would not dare miss. Balance is very important and I know from personal experience that every part of your life is impacted without it. You work better and are better for your loved one when you are somewhat happy or content and balanced. Just to give you an idea as you make your own list, the following is my simple go-to list weekly escape or break options. Some of the things listed are daily, weekly, monthly or quarterly. You must find what frequency is most realistic for your schedule and home life. Some of the simple daily escapes can be a challenge if you have kids or an air tight schedule, but consider doing it before others wake up at the beginning of your day or at the end of your day after everyone is already sleep so that you can have that alone time. If you don't have distractions at home, you may just have an insane tight agenda. Find the time even if you have to sacrifice something else or sleep for 30 minutes less daily because this will help you short and long term. My personal "go-to" escape list follows:

Daily/Weekly/Monthly
- Prayer
- Meditation
- Yoga
- 30 minute, quiet walk alone
- Escape into a favorite magazine or book
- Candles and bubble or oil bath
- Jazz or classical music and me time
- Visit to the park
- Trying new recipes that included healthy food
- Baking a cake, cookies or brownies
- Scrapbook to uplift from good old memories
- Volunteer a charity or fundraiser for a couple hours

- Send Get Well cards to sick shut in list from church
- Journal
- Local fun event or outing
- Day trip
- Weekend get away

Quarterly / Annually
- Spa
- Retreat
- Vacation

You may not get to do all of these things consistently, but pick at least one item from the list. Do something on your list rotationally on a consistent basis enough to get out of just focusing on your challenges, problems or work. Life is so much bigger than issues and work, but it is up to us to "create" the balance. We must live our life and make sure life doesn't live us. You can probably agree with me when I say that things will always be going on. Therefore, we must fit these little escapes of me time in because the clock is never going to stop and allow you "me time". Take it! I discovered this a few years ago because I got tired of being frustrated with myself, life and unexpected events that kept detouring my plans. Your life will be better the sooner you accept that you are never going to just have extra time to get around to doing something for yourself. It may not happen right away but you will eventually start working yourself into your own schedule more often. Then you will be more content or feel less frustrated because you have discarded

Life will never slow down for "me time". Take it!

unrealistic expectations. As you face various seasons, your routines change naturally but always schedule yourself on your own calendar. At one time, I slept only 3 -4 hours each night because I had such a full plate with work, graduate school, motherhood and family. Even back then, I made sure that I fit a little time in consistently for my journaling, scrapbooking, dancing, jazz wind down and candle bath on a regular monthly basis for my inexpensive "me time" and it did make a difference although it may not sound like a big deal. You may like something else that brings an "ahhh moment" to your routine but you owe whatever it is to yourself. As you are reading this, you probably agree but do not think it is possible or realistic. It will not be easy or overnight but it is possible and you will thank yourself later. You may find that when you have me time at least a few times a month, you have more patience, get less irritated, feel happier and feel less stress. You may experience these pleasant side effects because you are not in robot mode since you actually included regular, ongoing me time. If you are Superwoman or Diva that don't usually take consistent me time, get ready to feel guilty or uncomfortable constantly thinking of how much you could have done during the hour that you took out for yourself. It is natural and I encourage you to ignore the guilt and uneasy feeling until it goes away.

Where are you currently on the "me time" radar:

1. What do you currently do for yourself to escape?

   _____

   _____

2. How often do you take me time, and should you increase it?

_____

_____

3. What usually interfere with or delay your time?

_____

_____

4. What are you going to change to ensure adequate me time?

_____

_____

After you consistently find your "me time" escape, you will never look back because you will have a chance to see the positive impact it has on your mood. If things are a challenge financially, do not use that as an excuse to not do you. I listed a few examples of "me time" that do not require a penny. Consistent exercise (just walking 30 minutes) is definitely one of the "me time" options at least three times a week which will make a huge difference in your life if you are not already consistently working out. Furthermore, according to U.S. Department of Health and Human Services, consistent exercise lower risks of strokes by at least 27%, reduces diabetes by 50%, reduces higher blood pressure by 40%, lower the risk of colon/breast cancer 40-60%, decrease risk of Alzheimer's by 40% and help with treating depression.

Consistent exercise has endless positive effects on everyone. The summary chart below explains further.

Compared to an inactive person
(30 minutes of exercise or less per week)

1.5 hours of exercise per week	**20% lower risk** of premature death
3 hours of exercise per week	**27-28%** lower risk
5 hours of exercise per week	**33-34%** lower risk

**Exercise must be moderate intensity or greater.

U.S. Department of Health and Human Services

If you find yourself consistently taking me time and exercising but still cannot seem to get out of a rut or even find yourself in some type of depression, please do not ignore it. We all experience some type of depression throughout life, but it is usually short term or event related depression. If you find yourself in depression or unusual challenges for an extended period of time, you should talk to a professional because you deserve to be at peace and happy. However you might simply need a little temporary help to get to the root of what may be going on and identify solutions or techniques to take charge of finding your way back to content or happy. U.S. Department of

Health and Human Services defines depression as a serious growing medical illness; it's not something that you have made up in your head. It's more than just feeling "down in the dumps" or "blue" for a few days. It's feeling "down" and "low" and "hopeless" for weeks at a time.

Major Depressive Episode Symptoms
Cited by Psych Central Staff

A person who suffers from a major depressive episode must either have a depressed mood or a loss of interest or pleasure in daily activities consistently for at **least a 2 week period**. This mood must represent a change from the person's normal mood; social, occupational, educational or other important functioning must also be negatively impaired by the change in mood. A major depressive episode is also characterized by the presence of 5 or more of these symptoms:

- Depressed mood most of the day, nearly every day, as indicated by either subjective report (e.g., feeling sad or empty) or observation made by others (e.g., appears tearful). (In children and adolescents, this may be characterized as an irritable mood.)
- Markedly diminished interest or pleasure in all, or almost all, activities most of the day, nearly every day
- Significant weight loss when not dieting or weight gain (e.g., a change of more than 5% of body weight in a month), or decrease or increase in appetite nearly every day.

- Insomnia (inability to sleep) or hypersomnia (sleeping too much)
- Fatigue or loss of energy nearly every day
- Feelings of worthlessness or excessive or inappropriate guilt nearly every day
- Diminished ability to think or concentrate, or indecisiveness, nearly every day
- Recurrent thoughts of death (not just fear of dying), recurrent suicidal ideation without a specific plan, or a suicide attempt or a specific plan for committing suicide

How to Help Yourself if You Are Depressed

According to the Center for Disease Control (CDC), depression causes people to feel exhausted, worthless, helpless, and hopeless. Such negative thoughts and feelings make some people feel like giving up. It is important to realize that these negative views are part of the depression and typically do not accurately reflect the situation. Negative thinking fades as treatment begins to take effect. In the meantime:

- Set realistic goals and assume a reasonable amount of responsibility.
- Break large tasks into small ones, set some priorities, and do what you can as you can.

- Try to be with other people and to confide in someone; it is usually better than being alone and secretive.
- Participate in activities that may make you feel better.
- Mild exercise, going to a movie, a ballgame, or participating in religious, social, or other activities may help.

- Expect your mood to improve gradually, not immediately. Feeling better takes time.

- It is advisable to postpone important decisions until the depression has lifted. Before deciding to make a significant transition–change jobs, get married or divorced–discuss it with others who know you well and have a more objective view of your situation.

- People rarely "snap out of" a depression. But they can feel a little better day by day.

- Remember, positive thinking will replace the negative thinking that is part of the depression and will disappear as your depression responds to treatment.

- Let your closest family and friends help you.

Even if depression does not apply to you, please share this with others. Many people within your own family, workplace, community and church mask their depression. If you are not dealing with clinical depression, you can create or turn your joy up starting now regardless of areas that make you unhappy at work and home. Make sure that you work this chapter's suggestions and identify a list that works for you. Life is precious and you cannot afford to allow coworkers, relatives or friends to steal your joy if they have problems that stress you out. Although this is easier said than done, if you get into the habit of consistently doing something (even small) for yourself on a regular basis, you will increase your joy in the midst of the hell around you.

Chapter 6 Quick Start Take Away

Identify what you will do for yourself regularly.

Identify the detractors in your life.

Identify how to avoid or eliminate detractors.

_____

_____

_____

_____

_____

_____

_____

_____

_____

_____

Chapter 7

Renew You

"Are you investing your energy wisely?"

Renew is to begin or take up again, restore or replenish, revive; reestablish or recover. Which applies to you? Know that it is your time right now! If you have read all chapters in this book journey, you have an outline of your plan and map to additional success or internal growth that you desire. Perhaps you read through this book without taking notes or answering questions and that is okay for now. But be sure to go back through to answer the questions because it will be essential to have your personalized answers at your fingertips. When and if you get off track, it will be your guide to jumping right back on path without having to figure out where and how to start over. Most of us delay repositioning ourselves because we do not have the energy or time to figure out where we left off, and what we need to do next. As sure as twelve months exist in each year, you will have situations knock you off your path. However, your plans, faith, sacrifice and work will lead to your Breakthrough. You may be closer than you think. Don't give up a month before your Breakthrough! It does not matter if you started and failed at past goals and/or plans. Start over again right now! Quit delaying your success and move out of your comfort zone.

Renew yourself wherever you have been feeling defeated, neglected, overwhelmed or lost. No matter what happened in your past, you have another chance right now to restore, replenish, revive, recover or reestablish yourself. You may feel overwhelmed or tired but I hope that as you conclude this book you began to have zest, a flame or inspiration.

What is it that you need to renew? Perhaps you are just stuck in a rut, going in circles or feel like you have hit a dead end. Maybe it is something more specific and recent like family problems, divorce, difficult or troubled child, drama with friends, finances, school stress, workplace

> *You are only accountable for yourself. It is up to others to play their position.*

politics or something completely different. Know that once you have played your position, supported loved ones, took measures to get finances better, are doing your absolute best at school and/or work, all you can do is stand and pray. Progress takes time. Time is the answer for most situations and time usually passes very slow when you are anxious to see your situation turn around or loved ones get right. You can only be accountable and do all that you can within your power. Beyond that it is up to others to play their position. If they do not for some reason, pray about it as you continue on with your process for joy and peace within. Never give up on your situation getting better with finances, school, work, friends and family but do not wallow in it during the storm. Find your rainbow in the storm. If you wait on the storm to pass without finding a rainbow, it will drain the life out of you. Realistically, you will think about "work in progress" and feel sad or upset if it is taking awhile but you cannot allow it to paralyze you. Make a list of what you have done to improve whatever is still worrying you, write what you have done to improve it, figure out if there is anything else that you should do, do it and give it time to work itself out. Meanwhile, move forward and renew yourself. Not to sound harsh, but the reality is that unless you are a rare twin, you came into this world alone and you will also leave this world alone when your expiration day comes. We all are really only accountable and in control of self. Therefore, you cannot give other people too much control over your happiness. Get yours and don't let anyone take it, and do not allow any situation to take it too long. Realistically, we all will face bad or unexpected news which may break our hearts for quite a while. Even in those scenarios, we will find a way to have other joy in due time. The new joy or happiness will not compensate for a foreclosed house, repossessed car, heart break over a relative's behavior, broken relationship, deferred dream, tragedy, loss loved one or other devastating situation but it will help you move forward even if it is slow. Any movement is progress. Many people are facing situations that they can handle alone with time, resources and work. Depending on what the situation is, you may need help of trustworthy friends, family, experts or counselor to help you if it is a very serious situation. Regardless of what your situation is, you can and will renew yourself. Throughout this book, you worked on reflecting about your life, what you want, need, controllable situations, redefining and reinvesting. Now it is time to commit to renew yourself beyond past defeats, disappointments and self-conflicts. Let's explore your major strengths and opportunity areas. Also think about and identify what you have wanted to do for a while or something that you quit, delayed or avoided. Why? Are you thinking about restoring, replenishing, reviving, reestablishing or recovering from any of the following:

- College
  (college, graduate studies, doctorate)

- Career change

- Entrepreneurship

- Family

- Friends

- Physical appearance

- Internal Challenges

- Finances

If it is something that is not on the list above, you can still get it done by working on some self-probing questions. The answers are within you and what you are willing to do. Beware that life, situations, or procrastination will try to get your attention while you are in this last chapter that is the most important as you head into "your work". Remember that the workbook pages which you hopefully have completed, will help you pick up where you left off if something justifiably serious enough does take your attention away from your 3R journey. However, if no serious life event occurs, perhaps procrastination or stress about something else may try to delay you but don't fall for that again. Eliminate procrastination from your priorities and explore your stressors at a granular level.

Basically, procrastination is putting off essential task until a later time, and most of the time unessential tasks are done in lieu of the more critical ones. Although this procrastination definition seems pretty simple the effects of procrastination are not. Procrastination may be one of the biggest challenges you will have to overcome repeatedly. For some reason, we have an emotional reaction when we have to do something we don't want to do, don't enjoy doing, or are convinced we simply cannot do. Learning to acknowledge this reaction will not only make us aware that we may be procrastinating, but will also help us on our quest to stop procrastinating.

When you begin to think about today's society, there is less and less time in the day, so it is very important that we manage our time efficiently and limit procrastination as much as possible. If we do not get control of procrastination, it can lead to anxiety and that leads to self-inflicted stress. At a granular level, U.S. Department of Health and Human Services National Institutes of Health outlines stress as follows.

What exactly is stress?

Stress can be defined as the brain's response to any demand. Many things can trigger this response, including change. Changes can be positive or negative, as well as real or perceived. They may be recurring, short-term, or long-term and may include things like commuting to and from school or work every day, traveling for a yearly vacation, or moving to another home. Changes can be mild and relatively harmless, such as winning a race, watching a scary movie, or riding a rollercoaster. Some changes are major, such as marriage or divorce, serious illness, or a car accident. Other changes are extreme, such as exposure to violence, and can lead to traumatic stress reactions.

How does stress affect the body?

Not all stress is bad. At times, stress response can be life-saving in some situations. The nerve chemicals and hormones released during such stressful times, prepares one to face a threat or flee to safety. When you face a dangerous situation, your pulse quickens, you breathe faster, your muscles tense, your brain uses more oxygen and increases activity—all functions aimed at survival. In the short term, it can even boost the immune system. However, with chronic stress, those same nerve chemicals that are life-saving in short bursts can suppress functions that aren't needed for immediate survival. Your immunity is lowered and your digestive, excretory, and reproductive systems stop working normally. Once the threat has passed, other body systems act to restore normal functioning. Problems occur if the stress response goes on too long, such as when the source of stress is constant, or if the response continues after the danger has subsided.

How does stress affect your overall health?

There are at least three different types of stress, all of which carry physical and mental health risks:

- Routine stress related to the pressures of work, family and other daily responsibilities.
- Event related stress brought about by a sudden negative change, such as losing a job, divorce, or illness.
- Traumatic stress, experienced in an event like a major accident, war, assault, or a natural disaster where one may be seriously hurt or in danger of being killed.

The body responds to each type of stress in similar ways. Different people may feel it in different ways. For example, some people experience mainly digestive symptoms, while others may have headaches, sleeplessness, depressed mood, anger and irritability. People under chronic stress are prone to more frequent and severe viral infections, such as the flu or common cold, and vaccines, such as the flu shot, are less effective for them.

Of all the types of stress, changes in health from routine stress may be hardest to notice at first. Because the source of stress tends to be more constant than in cases of acute or traumatic stress, the body gets no clear signal to return to normal functioning. Over time, continued strain on your body from routine stress may lead to serious health problems, such as heart disease, high blood pressure, diabetes, depression, anxiety disorder, and other illnesses.

How to cope with stress?

The effects of stress tend to build up over time. Taking practical steps to maintain your health and outlook can reduce or prevent these effects. The following are some tips that may help you to cope with stress:

- Recognize signs of your body's response to stress, such as difficulty sleeping, increased alcohol and other substance use, being easily angered, feeling depressed, and having low energy.
- Set priorities-decide what must get done and what can wait, and learn to say no to new tasks if they are putting you into overload.
- Note what you have accomplished at the end of the day, not what you have been unable to do.

- Avoid dwelling on problems. If you can't do this on your own, seek help from a qualified mental health professional who can guide you.
- Exercise regularly-just 30 minutes per day of gentle walking can help boost mood and reduce stress.
- Schedule regular times for healthy and relaxing activities.
- Explore stress coping programs, which may incorporate meditation, yoga, tai chi, or other gentle exercises.
- Seek help from a qualified mental health care provider if you are overwhelmed, feel you cannot cope, have suicidal thoughts, or are using drugs or alcohol to cope.
- Get proper health care for existing or new health problems.
- Stay in touch with people who can provide emotional and other support. Ask for help from friends, family, and community or religious organizations to reduce stress due to work burdens or family issues, such as caring for a loved one.

Hopefully, you won't be distracted from "your time" that you deserve now that we have taken a coarse view at procrastination and stress, and how to cope with it better. Do not become overwhelmed by setting out to do too much. Tell yourself often, "I have enough time today to do everything that I really need to do." Focus on what you really need to do and avoid wasting time on fruitless tasks. The following questions may seem so basic but it is necessary as you **Renew**. It is necessary to value and cherish what is right as you attempt to build on for more progress and growth.

What do you appreciate about your life right now?

_____

_____

_____

_____

_____

What do you like about yourself internally?

_____

_____

_____

_____

What do you like about yourself externally?

_____

_____

_____

_____

_____

What are your strengths within your personal life?

_____

_____

_____

_____

_____

What are your strengths at work or school?

_____

_____

_____

_____

_____

If you could change one realistic thing in your life tomorrow, what would it be?

_____

_____

_____

_____

_____

What is your dream?

_____

_____

_____

_____

_____

Where do you want to be in 1 year and 5 years?

_____

_____

_____

_____

_____

What can you do to rise above your fear/procrastination?

_____

_____

_____

_____

After you finish this book, what are you going to do?

_____

_____

_____

_____

_____

Be honest and patient but remain consistent with your process to renew yourself. Depending on what you are trying to achieve, you need to pick what is most applicable to you and give it an honest effort.

You owe it to yourself.

- Create, redefine and commit to your plan

- Reinvest time, energy and resources into yourself

- Renew in any area that is below your true potential

- Start or increase exercise routine as it helps to keep you healthy and positive

- Identify needed changes at home, work or internal

- Change routines to maximize your life

- Review and improve your finances and spending

- Improve your current eating habits

Please remember that you did not get to this page in your life in just a week or a month, and you will not change it in just a week or a month. Commit to the most important person in your life, which is yourself, to work your action plan consistently and give it time. If life knocks you off of your action plan, just pick up where you left off and do not think or self-talk negatively. What is more important than taking yourself to the next level with your inner peace, joy, goal or any other growth you seek?

Chapter 7 Quick Start Take Away

Identify what you want to renew.

Identify why you want to renew.

Identify your next steps with a realistic timeline.

_____

_____

_____

_____

_____

_____

_____

_____

_____

_____

_____

Redefine, Reinvest, Renew

_____

_____

_____

_____

_____

_____

_____

_____

_____

_____

_____

_____

_____

_____

_____

_____

Quick Start Progress Tracker

Chapter 1

- ☐ Identify and list prior accomplishments.
- ☐ Identify and list your "it" or "its".
- ☐ Identify your fears and obstacles.

Chapter 2

- ☐ Identify your what *(may be multiple)*.
- ☐ Identify your why *(may be multiple)*.
- ☐ Identify your who *(may be multiple)*.

Chapter 3

- ☐ Identify your need(s).
- ☐ Identify your want(s).
- ☐ Identify what you are willing to sacrifice.

Chapter 4

- ☐ Identify what changed, ended or expired in your life.
- ☐ Identify how it affects you and your daily life.
- ☐ Identify how you will reposition and overcome.

Chapter 5

- ☐ Identify what is in your control.
- ☐ Identify what and who you do not have control of.
- ☐ Identify solutions to deal with difficult situations.

Chapter 6

- ☐ Identify the detractors in your life.
- ☐ Identify how to avoid or eliminate detractors.
- ☐ Identify what you will do for yourself regularly.

Chapter 7

- ☐ Identify what you want to renew.
- ☐ Identify why you want to renew.
- ☐ Identify your next steps and a realistic timeline.

Resource Guide
&
Helpful Tips

Career

Education

Family

Financial

Medical

*The following phone numbers and websites are provided because they are helpful public resources. This information does not serve as a personal referral or guarantee of any kind. National public sources are listed for your convenience as you move forward. Information is independent and subject to change.

💰 CREDIT REPORTS & DEBT 💰

Equifax
P.O. Box 105496
Atlanta, GA 30348-5496
800-685-1111
www.equifax.com

Experian
P.O. Box 2014
Allen, TX 75013
888-EXPERIAN
www.experian.com

TransUnion
P.O. Box 1000
Chester, PA 19022
800-888-4213
www.transunion.com

Annual Credit Report
www.annualcreditreport.com

EDUCATION SOURCES

Today, education is in a "no excuses" era. Flexible schools programs exist to fit anyone's lifestyle. Education requires temporary sacrifice and dedications for a permanent pay-off. Several grants, scholarships and loans are available to assist you. **Your education is a self-investment that opens the doors to more opportunities!** Are you worth it? Is your child worth it?

College Board
212-713-8000
www.collegeboard.com

College 411
800-505-4732
www.gacollege411.org

Financial Aid-Grants, Scholarships & Loans
800-433-3243
www.studentaid.ed.gov

National Association for the Education of Children
800- 424-2460
www.naeyc.org

U.S. Department of Education
800-872-5327
www.ed.gov

EMPLOYMENT SOURCES

America's Job Bank
877-889-5627
www.ajb.org

Department of Labor
877-872-5627

www.doleta.gov

Glassdoor
www.glassdoor.com

Head Hunter
www.headhunter.net

Indeed
www.indeed.com

Monster Jobs
www.monster.com

Simple Hired
www.simplyhired.com

USA Jobs
www.usajobs.opm.gov

HOME BUYING SOURCES

Bankrate.com
www.bankrate.com

E-Loan
www.eloan.com

Homefair
www.homefair.com

JOY Real Estate
Quentin Whitfield
864-297-3111 x207
www.joyrealestate.com

Lendingtree
www.lendingtree.com

Owners
www.owners.com

Smart Money
www.smartmoney.com

U.S. Department of Housing and Urban Development
www.HUD.gov

Zillow
www.zillow.com

Zip Realty
www.zipreality.com

HEALTH SOURCES

Free Clinics
(Locations throughout U.S.)
www.freeclinics.us

Affordable Healthcare

www.obamacareusa.org

Healthfinder

www.healthfinder.gov

Insure Kids Now
877-543-7669
www.insurekidsnow.gov

Healthcare Marketplace
www.healthcaremarketplace.com

Ovarian Cancer National Alliance
www.ovariancancer.org

Teal Butterflies Awareness
www.tealbutterflies.org

U.S. Dept. of Health and Human Services
(Medical Assistance and Counseling Information)
877-696-6775
www.hhs.gov

OTHER HELPFUL SOURCES

Child Care Information Center
800-616-2242
www.nccic.org

Every Woman's Fashions
404-626-9686

Legal – Do It Yourself Solutions
800-728-3555
www.nolo.com

Small Business Counselors to America
800-634-0245
www.score.org

Families First Transparenting
404-853-2864
www.transparenting.com

Butler New Media - Websites
678-235-4129
www.butlernewmedia.com

Your Art by Prince
(Mobile Art Gallery)
404-641-2343

Your Breakthrough
877-907-3888
www.yourbreakthrough.org

HOTLINES

www.allaboutcounseling.com

Abuse – (Child, Domestic or Sexual): 800-799-7233

Alzheimer's Association Hotline: 800-621-0379

Cancer Information Service: 800-422-6237

Child Abuse Hotline: 800-422-4453

Covenant House Hotline: 800-999-9999

Crisis Hotline: 800-448-3000

Disease Control: 800-458-5231

Elder Abuse Hotline: 800-252-8966

Mental Health Association: 800-969-6642

Missing Children Network: 800-235-3535

Parent Hotline: 800-840-6537

Poison Control Any Kind of Substance: 800-662-9886

Rape Crisis Hotline: 800-656-4673

Runaway Switchboard: 800-621-4000

Suicide Prevention and Crisis Hotline: 800-448-3000

RESOURCES

Corley, Tom, *Rich Habits-The Daily Success Habits of Wealthy Individuals,* p17

Edmond Jr, Alfred, *Money Matters,* p 87

Howard, Clark, *Personal Finance & Budgeting,* p86

Orman, Suzie, *Online Finance Tools-Debt Eliminator,* p85

Winfrey, Oprah, *What I Know for Sure,* p73

Also by LaShell Williams

Your Breakthrough on the Other Side
(Workbook pages and resource guide included)

ISBN   978-1-61584-607-8
$14.99

Single Mother Breakthrough
7 Proven Life Changing Steps to Success

ISBN   1-4243-1071-7
$9.99

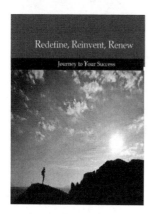

Redefine, Reinvent, Renew
Journey to Your Success

ISBN   978-0-9965422-0-3
$14.99